DO I HAVE TO GO TO SCHOOL TODAY?

Squib Measures Up!

Written and Illustrated by Larry Shles

For Matt —
just as you are!

Larry Shles '02

JALMAR PRESS

Jalmar Press
Permissions Department
P.O. Box 1185
Torrance, California
(310) 816-3085 Fax: (310) 816-3092 e-mail: blwjalmar@worldnet.att.net
Library of Congress Cataloging-in-Publication Data

Shles, Larry.
Do I Have To Go To School Today

Summary: Squib dreads going to school.
He daydreams about all the reasons
he has not to go. In the end, he decides
to go because his teacher accepts
him "Just as he is!"

[1. Fables. 2. Owls — Fiction. 3. Self-esteem — School]
I. Title. II. Title: Do I Have To Go To School Today.
Library of Congress Catalog Card Number: 89-84062
ISBN 0-915190-62-1

Printed in the United States of America

Cloth   P   Pbk. AL 10 9

To Esther, a teacher of my youth
and
Mildred, a mentor in my middle years

Books in the Squib Series by Larry Shles

Moths & Mothers, Feathers & Fathers

Do I Have To Go To School Today?

Hoots & Toots & Hairy Brutes

Aliens In My Nest

Hugs & Shrugs

Another Book by Larry Shles

Scooter's Tail of Terror

DO I HAVE TO GO TO SCHOOL TODAY?

Squib Measures Up!

Do I have to go to school today?
Moaned Squib, his stomach queasy.
Do I have to go to school today?
I feel a wee bit wheezy.

I'm afraid to go to school today,
That yellow monster might eat me!
It'll open its jaws and slurp me down
And in front of school secrete me.

The building's huge, the halls a maze.
I can't always find my room.
Yesterday I lost my way
And met with fright and doom.

Left, then right, then up the stairs,
I was sure I knew the path.
I strode with sureness through the door...

...And met with the older kids' wrath.

Hey punk, they said, get out of here!
This isn't the nursery school.
We're the big kids, tough and smart
And not to mention cool.

They stared at me with eyes ablaze.
They laughed and called me names.
Do I have to go to school today?
I'll stay home. We'll play some games!

Reading makes no sense to me,
The words could be from Mars.
The pages keep on piling up,
Reaching onward toward the stars.

I can hardly pick my textbook up,
It's like a wall a mile high.
I'll never finish what I start,
I'm afraid to even try.

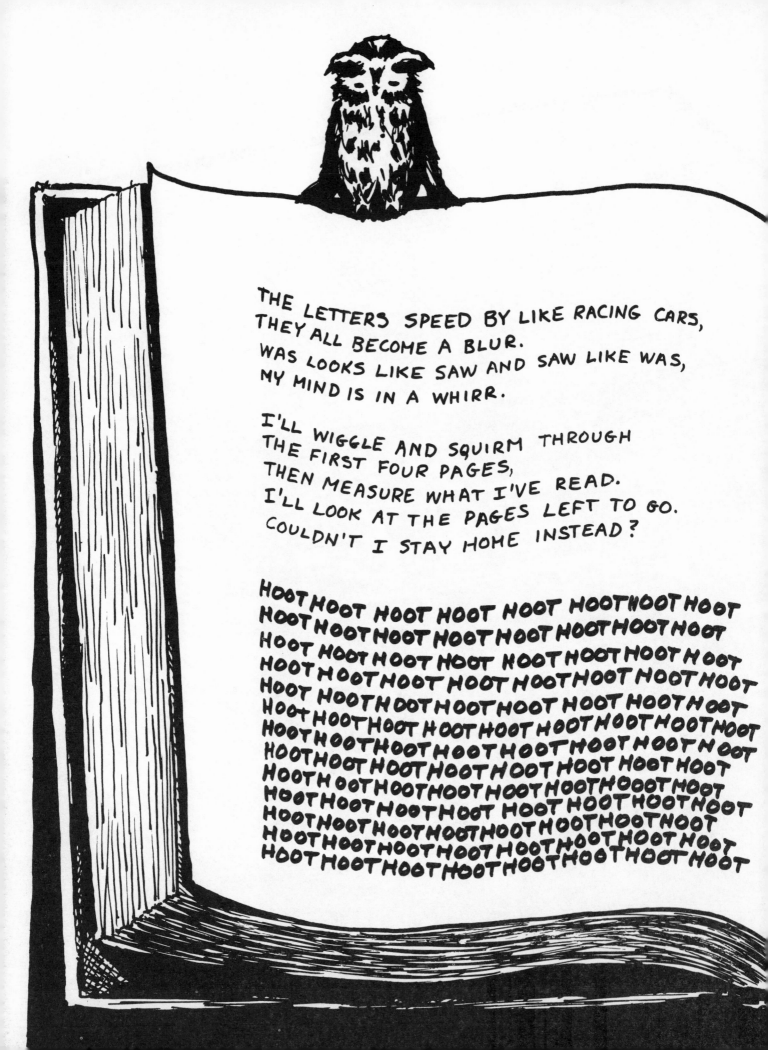

THE LETTERS SPEED BY LIKE RACING CARS,
THEY ALL BECOME A BLUR.
WAS LOOKS LIKE SAW AND SAW LIKE WAS,
MY MIND IS IN A WHIRR.

I'LL WIGGLE AND SQUIRM THROUGH
THE FIRST FOUR PAGES,
THEN MEASURE WHAT I'VE READ.
I'LL LOOK AT THE PAGES LEFT TO GO.
COULDN'T I STAY HOME INSTEAD?

HOOT HOOT HOOT HOOT HOOT HOOTHOOT HOOT
HOOT HOOT HOOT HOOT HOOT HOOT HOOT HOOT
HOOT HOOT HOOT HOOT HOOT HOOT HOOT HOOT
HOOT HOOT HOOT HOOT HOOT HOOT HOOT HOOT
HOOT HOOT HOOT HOOT HOOT HOOT HOOT HOOT
HOOT HOOT HOOT HOOT HOOT HOOT HOOT HOOT
HOOT HOOT HOOT HOOT HOOT HOOT HOOT HOOT
HOOT HOOT HOOT HOOT HOOT HOOT HOOT HOOT
HOOT HOOT HOOT HOOT HOOT HOOT HOOT HOOT
HOOT HOOT HOOT HOOT HOOT HOOT HOOT HOOT
HOOT HOOT HOOT HOOT HOOT HOOT HOOT HOOT
HOOT HOOT HOOT HOOT HOOT HOOT HOOT HOOT
HOOT HOOT HOOT HOOT HOOT HOOT HOOT HOOT
HOOT HOOT HOOT HOOT HOOT HOOT HOOT HOOT

Arts and crafts is most rewarding,
Though now and then I blow it.
From my desk I snatch my stuff
And around my chair I throw it.

Paper mache is a total blast,
My work goes fast, then faster.
I'm soon entombed in glue and glop,
I cast my own disaster.

Fingerpaint can be unsightly
As onto the paper it goes.
But I become the work of art
With green cheeks and beak and toes.

Oh, by the way, I got an "A"
For a moose I made in art.
I never worked with clay before,
I was timid at the start.

Once I started I forgot my fear
As the moose began to show.
With its antlers huge and curly tail,
Excitement began to grow!

It got an "A" for imagination,
To me it's just a moose.
They said my style is one of a kind.
Do they mean like Dr. Seuss?

Cursive!

Do I have to go to school today?
My cursive is far from cautious.
My words look more like a carnival ride.
I finish whoozy and nauseous.

My j's like y's, my y's like z's,
My b's are a total mess.
When I connect the letters up,
I make words that you can't guess.

Foiled again

Gooey gum and sandwich crumbs,
Globs of glue and last month's stew,
Swarms of bats and pesty gnats —
My desk looks more like a zoo!

A kid reached in to swipe my lunch,
In a blink he was gone from sight.
The creature that lurks within this gunk
Had swallowed the guy in one bite!

My classmates vanished, one by one,
Into this horrid pit.
Do I have to go to school today?
There are safer places to sit!

P.E. is tough; dodgeball's a fright.
The gym's a place I dread.
Kids grab the ball and snarl at me,
Then whomp me in the head.

The ultimate challenge is basketball,
My height is not way up there.
Dribbles and pivots, jams and jumps?
I can't even dodge the footwear!

Last week the ball was passed to me,
The hoop was in my vision.
I flung it upward with a gasp,
I thought it a good decision.

The ball rose up, the net awaited,
I stood there with a flair.
The ball came down and knocked me
    senseless.
All I had swished was the air!

Today is music. You should hear me sing.
I'm not a tenor or bass.
What I release is an unearthly screech,
Like an owl toe from outer space.

The notes go up, my voice goes down.
Besides, I forget the words.
The beat goes on as I lag behind
With a scream that turns cream into curds.

I'm tired of playing the trumpet
And the band is much too noisy.
A trombone blast from the row behind
Propelled me to New Joisy.

I toppled into the tuba,
I couldn't stand the feeling.
The climax came with a mighty belch
That launched me through the ceiling.

The nurse called me from class last week
To check for fleas and ticks.
While I was there, she found much more.
It's the way she gets her kicks.

Under my wing, an inchworm nest
Had grown to large dimension.
I wish I hadn't learned of it.
I don't need the extra tension!

I'm short for my age. My life is tough.
I can't even fly or hoot.
The last thing I need, believe you me,
Is an inchworm suit to boot.

Dew eye half two go too school twoday?
Spelling makes me blew.
There, their and they're: where, wear and
  ware,
I'm trapped in an alphabet stew.

I doodled all over my spelling test,
From vowels I created my face.
I drew me in a consonant soup,
It wasn't the time or the place.

I got a "D" on my spelling exam,
Though I really can't complain.
It got an "A" as a project in art,
But to spell "art" gives me a pain.

My science projects have always flopped,
I can't even grow mold on bread.
In seven weeks my bread was bare,
The fuzz had covered me instead!

The beans I planted in the towel
Were supposed to sprout and grow.
I waited for the leaves and stems.
I had hoped some roots would show.

The beans turned mushy, soft and limp,
With strange mounds of blacks and greens.
After fourteen weeks my bread was bare...
The mold had spread to my beans.

I started over with two snakes,
To one I fed some mice.
The other got our lunchroom food ...
The results were far from nice.

The mouse-fed snake ate the fifth grade class,
The other could not awake.
After thirty weeks my bread was bare ...
The mold had snacked on my snake.

Mold covered my desk, my teacher too,
The sight of my room you'd dread.
The only thing without the goo —
You guessed it — it was my bread.

The science fair was cancelled last year,
I know it might sound cruel.
After forty weeks I ate my bread . . .

…The mold had devoured my school!

The lunchroom's gross. The food tastes bad.
The worms are stuck together.
The pizza's piled with octopus eyes,
The crust chews more like leather.

Muskrat mousse and mouse-kabobs,
The menu's not like mom's.
And if you take the snake souffle,
You'd swear you downed some bombs.

①

$$\frac{1}{4} + \frac{3}{7} + \frac{5}{11} + \frac{1}{3} + \frac{7}{8} + \frac{11}{12} = \underrightarrow{}$$

②

🦉 ✕ 🦉 = 🦉

③

$$373 \overline{)9765324672.000000} \quad 26180495.$$

746
2305
2238
673
373
3002
2984
1846
1492
3547
3357
1902
1965

I have to take a test in math,
My chances are appalling.
I'm sure I won't get any right,
I don't want my teacher calling.

I'll stare at the problems on the test,
Then try to work them out.
I'll chew on my pencil and scratch my head
And then begin to pout.

I'm hardly partial to fractions
And division takes too long.
Multiplying is terrifying,
My answers are often wrong.

Perhaps I should stay home today,
I feel a bit more wheezy.
It's hard for me to measure up,
Nothing at school is easy.

My cheeks are green, my wings are fuzz,
I can't write a perfect paper.
I'm swamped and scared, my weakness is
 bared
As my strengths turn into vapor.

There's a lot of things I do quite well,
Though you'd never know it from school.
The ideas I have are really great,
But they don't follow any rule.

Like a story I wrote about my brother.
He's difficult to render.
He's slightly weird and all mixed up,
So I drew him in a blender.

My teacher loved my story
And loved my drawings too.
She said I was quite a writer.
She'll read anything I do.

She bound my story into a book
And put it on display.
She shared it with the principal
And named me "Author For The Day"!

Wait! I'll dress and catch the bus,
My mind has suddenly changed!
With all my whines and groans and gripes,
I seem to be deranged.

I'll go to school and try to read,
I want to draw and write.
I'll face her with my shining eyes
And listen with all my might.

I can't wait to get to school today,
I just thought of her this minute.
She greets me at the classroom door
With a warmth that draws me in it.

She's my teacher, kind and patient,
She knows I'm not a whiz.
She takes me by the wing and smiles …

… She accepts me just as is!

DO I HAVE TO GO TO SCHOOL TODAY?
LEADER'S GUIDE

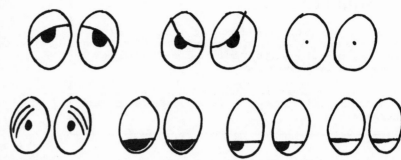

Copy the drawing of Squib on the left. Then choose eyes on the right to give him the feeling you want him to have. You may experiment and create eyes with different expressions. Then write about or discuss a time in your life when you felt that way.

1) It is helpful if we can emphasize the positive side of any situation. Write a portion of a Squib story that uses the refrain, "I can't wait to get to school today... ."

2) Squib does not recognize his positive qualities until his teacher points them out. Do you have positive qualities that you ordinarily overlook. What are they?

1) Make a list of the things that go wrong at school for Squib; then make a list of things that go right for him. Why do you think his teacher was enough to change his mind about school even though being there was so difficult? Do you think this was a realistic ending to the story?

2) Write about the most important adult who has ever been in your life. Does that person have anything in common with Squib's teacher?

3) Compare Squib's experiences in each of the five Squib volumes. What themes are common to all books? On the basis of these books, what do you think the author is like?

The Continuing Saga of Squib the Owl

"Shles has caught the spirit of the fledgling...an extremely effective portrayal of the child we all once were. Bravo to him for giving us Squib — long may he live and grow!" — **Doris Weber, St. Louis Globe-Democrat.**

"Squib allows readers to be vulnerable and invites them to trust, to dare, and to triumph." — **Marian Junge, Teacher and Librarian.**

Moths & Mothers, Feathers & Fathers
A Story About a Tiny Owl Named Squib

Larry Shles

Squib is a tiny owl who cannot hoot or fly, neither can he understand his feelings. He must face the frustration, fear, and loneliness that we all must face at different times in our lives. Struggling with these feelings, he searches, at least, for understanding.

8 1/2 x 11, 72 pages, paperback, illustrations.
ISBN 0-915190-57-5

Aliens In My Nest
Squib Meets the Teen Creature

Larry Shles

In *Aliens in my Nest*, Squib comes home from summer camp to find that his older brother, Andrew, has turned into a snarly, surly, defiant, and non-communicative adolescent. Friends, temperament, dress, entertainment, thoughts about authority, room decor, eating habits, music likes and dislikes, isolation, internal and external conflict and many other areas of change are dealt with in this remarkably illustrated book.

8 1/2 x 11, 80 pages, trade paperback, illustrations.
ISBN 0-915190-49-4

Hoots & Toots & Hairy Brutes
The Continuing Adventures of Squib

Larry Shles

Squib — who can only toot — sets out to learn how to give a mighty hoot. His attempts result in abject failure. Every reader who has struggled with life's limitations will recognize his struggles and triumphs in the microcosm of Squib's forest world. A parable for all ages from eight to eighty.

8 1/2 x 11, 72 pages, paperback, illustrations.
ISBN 0-915190-56-7

Do I Have To Go To School Today?
Squib Measures Up!

Larry Shles

Squib dreads the daily task of going to school. In this volume, he daydreams about all the reasons he has not to go. But, in the end, Squib convinces himself to go to school because his teacher accepts him "Just as he is!"

8 1/2 x 11, 64 pages, trade paperback, illustrations
ISBN 0-915190-62-1

Hugs & Shrugs
The Continuing Saga of Squib

Larry Shles

Squib feels incomplete. He has lost a piece of himself. He searches everywhere only to discover that his missing piece has fallen in and not out. He becomes complete again once he discovers his own inner-peace.

8 1/2 x 11, 72 pages, trade paperback.
ISBN 0-915190-47-8 $7.95

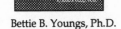